We Elect a President

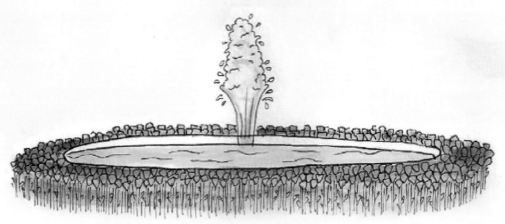

We Elect a President

The Story of Our Electoral College

Tara Ross

Illustrated by
Kate E. Cooper

With special contributions by Emma Ross

COLONIAL PRESS, L.P.
Dallas, Texas
www.colonialpressonline.com

Acknowledgments

I owe many thanks to several librarians, teachers, parents, and academics who helped me with this book. I usually write for adults! Creating an illustrated book such as this one was a different kind of challenge. I am grateful to Barbara Allen, Amy Davis, Trent England, Heather Goldman, Kristin Jones, Elizabeth Kovacs, Terry O'Daniel, Kim Ray, and Tiffany Willett, each of whom had helpful advice on how to write in this genre. (Or just let me run the book by the kids in their lives!) I am so grateful for everyone's help.

COLONIAL PRESS, L.P.
6125 Luther Ln., No. 280
Dallas, Texas 75225
www.colonialpressonline.com

First Edition

ISBN: 978-0-9770722-3-1
LCCN: 2016939186

Printed in the United States of America

From the girls in the Ross family
to the boys in the Ross family,
with much love

Tara & Emma

To my parents, Susan and Chris,
and my siblings, William and Charlotte,
with lots of love

Kate

A Note for Teachers and Parents

The Electoral College is often misunderstood—and perhaps especially hard to explain to our children. I hope this book provides an easy introduction to the subject. I expect that the book will be used by a variety of ages, so I've included sections intended to help not only those who want harder material but also those who need easier explanations.

Several of the pages include a section called "Emma's Corner." This section is aimed at younger readers who might need concrete examples of some of the more nebulous concepts in this book. "Emma" is a real person—my daughter, who will be entering fourth grade as this book is released. Her generation is my target audience, and I've considered Emma's input critical throughout the book-writing process. She helped generate all of the ideas for her "corner." I hope they are helpful for those of you with younger children. By contrast, some pages include "The Founders' Corner." This section is intended to help those who want a jumping-off point for more discussion or research. I also hope it helps older readers to hear how the Founders expressed some of these ideas in their own words.

This book goes to press in the midst of an unusually contentious presidential primary season, so it is worth noting that the parties' nomination processes are completely separate from the Electoral College and the general election in November. The party nomination processes are a creation of political parties and the states. The Electoral College has its roots in the Constitution. To the degree that our primary process is broken, perhaps we can learn from the Electoral College. Can our Founders' principles be better reflected in the political primaries?

Finally, I am thankful for my illustrator. As this book goes to press, Kate Cooper is just graduating from high school and preparing to enter college. This book was completed on a tight timeline, and Kate gave many hours of her final high school semester to help. I feel blessed to have found a student with so much talent!

I love the final product and hope that you do, too.

Tara

George Washington was the first President of the United States. Did you ever wonder: Who decided that he would be President?

Americans chose him! But we used our own, very special method of choosing Presidents. It's called the Electoral College.

We've used this system to pick all our Presidents. No other country has a process quite like ours.

In some countries, everyone votes for President, and the person who gets the most votes wins. Sometimes, they have to hold more than one election because no one gets enough votes on the first try. In other countries, the heads of state are chosen by their version of Congress. In countries led by dictators, citizens may not get to vote for President at all. Some countries have Kings instead of Presidents!

Americans have our very own system. We need something special because our country is so big and we have so many different states and regions.

One special feature of our election process is that it happens in two parts. First, people vote in their states. Next, states get a turn to vote.

Why did our Founders—men like George Washington, James Madison, and Alexander Hamilton—set it up this way? Isn't it kind of weird to let states vote? Wouldn't it be easier to hold one big national election among the people and leave the states out of it?

Well, maybe it is a bit odd to let states vote, but the Founders had learned a lot from their experiences during the American Revolution. After all, they'd barely escaped from a British King who was really pushing Americans around! They knew they needed to create something different and unique. They did not want the new American government to be a bully, just like the King.

Do you know why Americans fought the Revolution in the first place? A long time ago, America used to be a part of Great Britain. Then the British government tried to tax us, even though we were all the way across the ocean. Americans had a pretty big problem with that!

Why should the British government get to tax Americans? The people in America didn't get to vote for any of the leaders over there!

Americans thought they should get to vote before anyone tried to tax them. Otherwise, the British government would turn into a big bully, treating British citizens in England (who could vote) better than the American colonists (who couldn't vote).

Emma's Corner

One day, my class was voting on what book to read. We had four choices, and I voted for *Charlotte's Web*. Fortunately, *Charlotte's Web* won. I'm so glad the teacher let everyone have a say! What if the teacher had said something like: Only people with blonde hair get to vote? Wouldn't that be unfair to everyone else when they all had to listen to the book, chosen by only the blonde kids?

The Declaration of Independence

We hold these Truths to be self-evident, that all Men are created equal, that they are endowed by their Creator with certain unalienable Rights, that among these are Life, Liberty, and the Pursuit of Happiness—That to secure these Rights, Governments are instituted among Men, deriving their just Powers from the Consent of the Governed, that whenever any Form of Government becomes destructive of these Ends, it is the Right of the People to alter or to abolish it, and to institute new Government . . . .

Of course, the Founders did more than just look to our own history in America. They also studied the history of other nations. They knew what had worked (and what had not worked) in other countries.

They learned something! A **DEMOCRACY**, in which people simply vote for what they want, doesn't always work. An old example explains why.

Pretend that two wolves and a sheep decide to vote on what to have for dinner. Well, do you know what wolves eat? They eat sheep!

The sheep will always lose that vote and be eaten for dinner. Right?

The Founders knew that it's not enough just to let people vote. A fair government will make sure that smaller groups of people (like the sheep!) can protect themselves from bullies who could outvote them.

The Founders' Corner

*Perhaps the most important thing to understand about our Constitution is that the Founders were not trying to create a **pure** (or simple) democracy. They wanted to be self-governing, of course. They had just fought a Revolution partly because they had no representation in Parliament! On the other hand, they knew their history: Pure democracies have a tendency to implode. The wolves are always tyrannizing the sheep.*

"A democracy is a volcano, which conceals the fiery materials of its own destruction."
– Fisher Ames
With his help, Massachusetts ratified the Constitution!

"[D]emocracy never lasts long. It soon wastes, exhausts, and murders itself. There never was a democracy yet that did not commit suicide."
– John Adams
Second President of the United States

"A simple democracy . . . is one of the greatest of evils."
– Benjamin Rush
He signed the Declaration of Independence!

"Pure democracy . . . is very subject to caprice and the madness of popular rage."
– John Witherspoon
He signed the Declaration of Independence, too!

After they were done learning from history, the Founders did one more thing: They remembered that people are not perfect. People make mistakes! Some people are bad. Some people don't mean to be bad, but when they are put in charge, they begin to think that it is really fun to boss people around!

The new American government would need to protect everyone in case a bad or very bossy person gets elected by accident.

Emma's Corner

Have you noticed how some kids start being bossy as soon as the teacher leaves the room? And when the teacher comes back, they pretend that the rude, bossy behavior never happened? No one likes to be around a bully. Imagine that the Constitution is like the teacher. As long as it is around, it is harder for Presidents and Congressmen to be bullies.

Our Founders wanted to create something new that would keep all these lessons in mind: First, the people should always be in charge of their own government. The government should never have any power except when the people decide it's okay.

The Founders' Corner

The Founders wanted hurdles to stop (or at least to slow down) irrational, bare, or emotional majorities. Minority political interests should be protected from the tyranny of the majority. The Founders thus created a Constitution that combines democracy (self-governance) with federalism (states acting on their own behalves) and republicanism (encouraging deliberation and compromise). The various checks and balances in our Constitution protect our liberty.

"To secure the public good and private rights against the danger of such a [majority] faction, and at the same time to preserve the spirit and the form of popular government, is then the great object to which our inquiries are directed."
— James Madison
A federalist republic, he concluded, protects individual rights better than a democracy.

"A Republic, if you can keep it."
— Benjamin Franklin
He was asked what the Constitutional Convention had produced.

The opinion of the people should always matter! They should get to vote and have a say. The Founders knew this was really important in a free country.

On the other hand, the Founders knew that a simple voting system would not be enough. They had to find a way to make things just a little more fair for small groups of voters. These small groups might still lose elections sometimes, but it shouldn't be so bad that they are like the sheep that gets eaten for dinner just because it lost a vote.

The Founders would use big phrases to describe this problem. How can they avoid the **TYRANNY OF THE MAJORITY** but still allow the people to be **SELF-GOVERNING**?

With all these problems, it was also really hard to find a fair system for electing Presidents. Our Founders had lots of debates about it when they were writing our Constitution.

Some people thought we should just hold one big national election for President, but that idea scared the people from small states. They thought the big states would outvote them and get to choose the President all the time.

Other people thought that we should let Congress pick the President. That seemed like a bad idea, too, though. Wouldn't Congress just end up bossing the President around? And no one knew what Congress was going to look like, anyway.

For a long time, no one could agree on anything!

The Founders' Corner

"The most populous States by combining in favor of the same individual will be able to carry their points."
— Charles Pinckney of South Carolina

*He didn't want one big national election
because small states would be ignored.*

"I do not, gentlemen, trust you. If you possess the power, the abuse of it could not be checked; and what then would prevent you from exercising it to our destruction?"
— Gunning Bedford, Jr. of Delaware

Small state delegate talking to large state delegates!

"He will be the mere creature of the [Legislature]: if appointed & impeachable by that body."
— Gouverneur Morris of Pennsylvania

*He did not want Congress to order
the President around!*

"[T]he appointment of the Executive should either be drawn from some source, or held by some tenure, that will give him a free agency with regard to the Legislature."
— James Madison of Virginia

*If Congress can control the President, Madison added, then it
would be "dangerous to public liberty."*

The Founders were still arguing about how to elect a President when they got caught up in a completely different disagreement.

What kind of Congress should we have? In other words, who gets to make laws in America?

Everyone already agreed that Congress should not get to make **ALL** the laws. The states could make most laws by themselves. Congress would make laws only in certain areas of national interest.

It was easy to agree on that part of it. But the states had more trouble agreeing on who gets to be in Congress.

The small states wanted a Congress in which every state would get the same number of votes. They were still very worried that the big states would pass laws to hurt the small states! But the large states disagreed. Shouldn't Virginia get more votes than tiny Delaware?

Fortunately, the Founders worked out a compromise.

They decided that Congress would be split in half! One part, the Senate, would be exactly like the small states wanted. The other part, the House of Representatives, would be exactly like the big states wanted.

Congress can make laws only when the Senate and House agree.

Then the Founders had another idea! If Congress could be half like the big states wanted and half like the small states wanted, couldn't the same thing work for choosing Presidents?

Yes! It could. And that's exactly what they decided to do. But how, exactly, did they make that work?

It turned out to be easier than you might think, but the Founders knew they would have to create something new and unique. They could not simply hold one big, national election among all the people. The states would need a turn, too.

Emma's Corner

Pretend you are running a lemonade stand with a friend. You want each glass to cost $1. Your friend wants each glass to cost 50 cents. The two of you simply can't agree! Finally, you realize that you can compromise: Each glass will cost 75 cents.

We call the election system that they created the "Electoral College." Isn't that kind of a funny name? It sounds like it should be a school or university, but it is not. It's just the name we use for our special way of electing Presidents.

Our special way of electing Presidents has two parts.

First, each state must decide which presidential candidate it likes best. Do you know how states make this decision? Easy! States ask their citizens to vote. On Election Day in November, **INDIVIDUAL PEOPLE** vote. They are telling their state which candidate they like best.

The candidate who wins the most votes in a state gets to be the choice of that state.

After that, each state asks a few people, called electors, to help with the second part of the election. These electors have already promised to vote for the person that their state wants. In December, a new election is held. In this election, **ELECTORS** cast votes for their states.

The December election is the one that decides who gets to be President. A President is elected if a majority of electors vote for him. That means he needs 270 votes because there are 538 electors.

George Washington was the choice of all the states in 1789!

Emma's Corner

In 2012, I watched my mom vote in Texas. I learned something cool. Did you know that your mom or dad isn't really voting for the presidential candidate? I thought my mom was voting for Mitt Romney or Barack Obama. She wasn't! It turns out that she was voting for regular Texans. If the Republican Texans got the most votes, Texas would vote for Romney. If the Democratic Texans got the most votes, Texas would vote for Obama.

Perhaps you won't be surprised to hear that big states get more electors than small states. They have more people! But small states always get at least three electors, no matter what.

This helps the small states, just a little. The Founders were hoping it would be just enough to keep them from being like the sheep who keeps getting outvoted by the wolves.

Emma's Corner

What state do you live in? Do you know how many electors your state has? I live in Texas, and my state has 38 electors. How did Texas get 38 votes and not some other number? Because Texas has 36 Congressmen and 2 Senators! Every state has the same number of electors as they have members of the House and Senate.

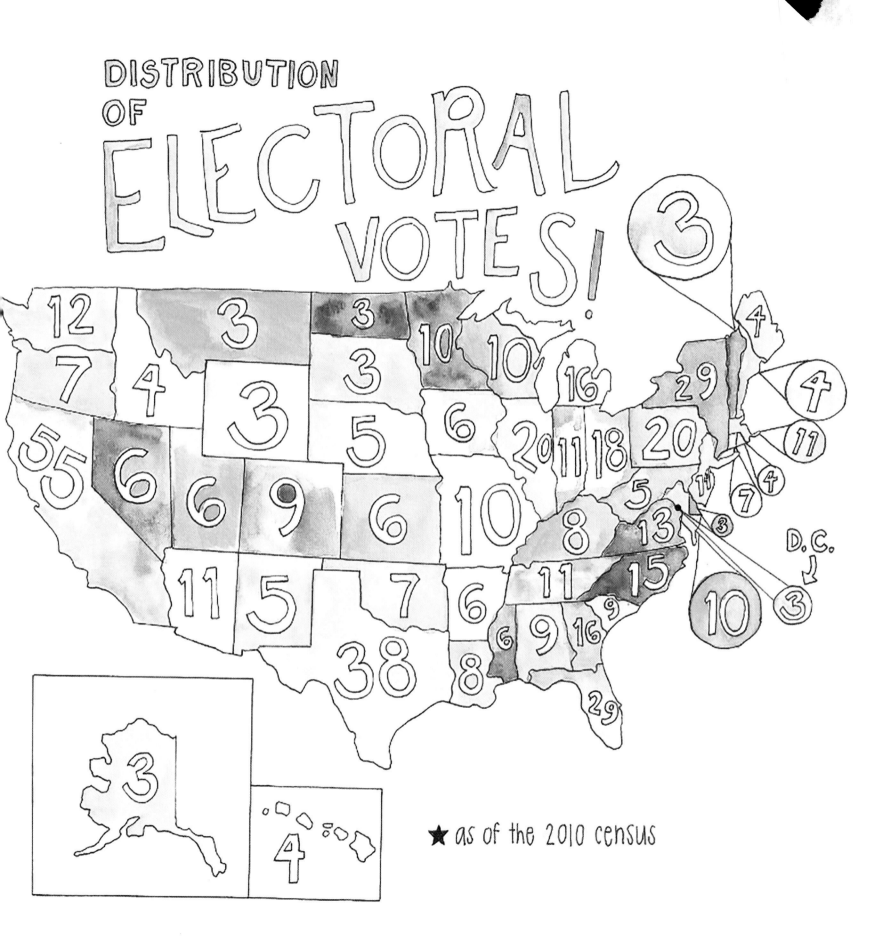

Every once in a while, Presidents are elected because they got the most **ELECTORS** to vote for them in December, even though they did not get the most **INDIVIDUAL PEOPLE** to vote for them in November. You might hear people say: "But that's not fair! Shouldn't the person with the most votes win?"

Actually, it is fair. But it helps if we remember some of the good things that happen today because of the Electoral College.

And it helps if we remember what a big, diverse place America is. Our country is full of so many different kinds of people—and our states are all sorts of different sizes.

Emma's Corner

One day, my mom told me to get into the car so we could run an errand. But I wanted to stay home and read! I was almost done with my book. I protested, but my mom made me hop in the car. I was disappointed and grumbled about how unfair she was being. Suddenly, the car stopped. I looked up. Then, I saw why she had brought me along. My mom had arranged a surprise sleepover with my best friend! I smiled and skipped inside. My mom's actions **FELT** unfair, but once I understood what she was doing, I realized that it really wasn't unfair at all.

Think about it. Some people live in big cities, while others live in small cities. Some people are teachers, but others work in coal mines or on farms. Some people are Christians. Others are Jews or Muslims.

What if a person could get elected President by getting all the people in big cities to vote for him? Wouldn't the people in small cities be worried that they were going to get eaten like the sheep?

Or what if a person could get elected President by getting doctors and lawyers to gang up on teachers and farmers? Would that be fair to the teachers and the farmers?

The Electoral College is the fairest system for our country because it makes presidential candidates think about lots of different kinds of people, in lots of different states.

When candidates forget this and focus too much on only one kind of voter, they always lose. They might get a lot of votes in one part of the country and win the November vote among **INDIVIDUALS**, but they won't have enough states to win the December vote among **ELECTORS**.

Emma's Corner

Pretend your school is electing a student body president. One candidate is from 6th grade and one is from 8th grade. There's just one problem: The 8th grade has 200 students! The 6th and 7th grades have less: only 180 people, total. Now imagine that the 8th grader makes a big promise: If he wins, he will make sure that 8th grade is always first in the lunch line! The entire 8th grade votes for him, but no one else does. He wins, 200 to 180. The 6th and 7th graders think the election is pretty unfair. Why can the 8th grader be so mean to the 6th and 7th grades and win anyway? Fortunately, no state can ever be like the 8th grade when we elect a President. The Electoral College doesn't let it happen.

The Electoral College protects the small states and the less populated areas of the country, but it does something else, too. It encourages Americans to work together. In order to win the Electoral College vote, a presidential candidate must remember the things that bring us together as Americans, rather than focusing on areas where we disagree or are upset.

What solutions work for the most people at the same time? What encourages Americans to remember our common history and our common values? If presidential candidates want to win many states, all at the same time, then they need to figure out the answers to these questions.

If we take time to see what has happened in the past, we discover that presidential candidates are most successful when they help people to get along. They do poorly when they make some groups of people really mad at the other groups.

Emma's Corner

Pretend that you need to make a banner for your school's volleyball team. You know exactly what you want to draw, and you have the colors all picked out. The banner is really big, though. You need help! You ask your friends, but they say no. They don't like your colors or the way you want to draw volleyballs. At first, you get pretty upset. Why won't anyone help? Finally, you decide to ask again. This time you say: "Why don't you draw the volleyballs your way, and I'll pick the spot to hang the banner. We'll use colors we both like." Your friends like this idea better and finally say yes. Soon everyone is pitching in to help.

The Electoral College once worked to unify the country when Americans **REALLY** did not want to be together!

After the Civil War, the Electoral College was one factor that forced North and South to start working together again.

Why? The Democrats were strongest in the South, and they could not win unless they figured out how to get some votes from the more Republican states in the North. In the same way, Republicans had to figure out how to compete with the Democrats. If the Democrats took even some of their voters, then they would lose the election.

In the end, Democrat Grover Cleveland finally figured out how to earn the trust of some northerners, and he was elected in 1884.

The Electoral College has one more benefit that might surprise you! It helps to stop bad guys from stealing elections.

Did you know that an election can be stolen? Elections are stolen when bad guys pretend to be someone else and vote for them. Or sometimes bad guys take people's votes and hide them so they can't get counted.

Don't you wish that someone could wave a magic wand and turn a bad guy into a good guy? In real life, no one has that kind of a magic wand, but the Electoral College does the next best thing:

It makes it harder for the bad guys to get away with their bad behavior. This only works because **BOTH** people and states get a turn to vote.

What good does it do to steal people's votes unless you know where to steal them?

Because of the Electoral College, the bad guys have to know, in advance, which state might have a close outcome. Then they have to figure out how to steal votes in that one state. If the bad guys know where to steal votes, then the good guys probably know, too. They will work hard to stop the bad guys!

Without the Electoral College, this wouldn't work. The bad guys could steal votes anywhere! In fact, they would just pick the place where it is easiest to be bad, and they would steal as many votes as they could in that city or state.

Emma's Corner

Have you ever been on an Easter egg hunt? Pretend that you are looking for Easter eggs in your house. Dozens of eggs are hidden in each room! No matter where you go, there is an egg to be found. You find a whole bunch of eggs very fast. Now, imagine a different Easter egg hunt: Fewer eggs are hidden, and they are all in only one room. You don't know which room has the eggs. By the time you figure it out, your brother and sister have figured it out, too. They are taking eggs before you can find them! It takes longer to find the eggs, and you don't get as many. Isn't it a lot easier to find the eggs when you know there will be many eggs in **EVERY** room, rather than a smaller number of eggs in only one room?

The idea for our Electoral College was completely new. Our Founders were looking for something that would let the majority rule, but that would also make sure that bullies weren't always voting to eat the sheep!

America is a huge country, and the President is the only person who is expected to represent people in every state and every city. We have many states, many regions, many industries, and many religious beliefs. But **EVERYONE** should have a voice when it is time to pick our President.

The Founders' Corner

"The mode of appointment of the Chief Magistrate of the United States is almost the only part of the system . . . which has escaped without severe censure . . . . I venture somewhat further, and hesitate not to affirm that if the manner of it be not perfect, it is at least excellent."

— Alexander Hamilton

He helped write the Constitution!

The Founders felt that they accomplished all these goals, and they were very proud of the "excellent" presidential election process that they'd created.

The Electoral College has served America well for many years. We can be just as proud of it as our Founders were.

Glossary

American Revolution: A war fought between Great Britain and the American colonies beginning in 1775. The American colonies won their freedom from Great Britain. We became our own country!

Candidate: A man or woman who is trying to get elected to a public office, such as President, Senator, or Governor.

Congress: The United States government is divided into three sections (usually called three "branches"): Executive, Legislative, and Judicial. Congress is the Legislative branch of our government. It makes the laws.

Constitution: A document containing the basic set of laws upon which a government is based. The United States Constitution created the United States government, so our government can have only the powers that the Constitution gives to it. The government may not create new powers for itself! The Constitution also contains a Bill of Rights, which expressly states the many rights that the people have kept for themselves. For example, Americans have the right to speak freely and to choose our own religion. The government cannot make those decisions for us.

Declaration of Independence: A document signed by 56 men, on behalf of the American colonies, in 1776. It declared the many reasons that Americans felt mistreated by Great Britain. Our Founders were letting the British know that we were choosing to separate. We were ready to be our own country!

Democracy: A self-governing society in which simple majorities rule. In other words, 51% of the people can always outvote the other 49%, even if they are voting to do something mean! In a democracy, the people sometimes vote for what they want directly. At other times, they elect representatives who are then expected to vote as the people want them to vote.

Dictator: Someone who rules a country without caring what the people think. He just does what he wants, even if it means forcing the people in his country into doing things they'd rather not do!

Elector: A person who has been selected to vote in a presidential election on behalf of his state. Electors are chosen by the voters on Election Day in November. They agree to vote for the choice of their states during the December election among the states.

Electoral College: The American system of electing Presidents. The phrase "Electoral College" is an informal name that has been used by many people for a long time, but the phrase does not appear in the Constitution.

Federalism: Governmental power is shared in America. The Constitution gives our national (federal) government some power, but the states keep the rest.

States are supposed to be able to make their own decisions in many areas, even if the federal government (or another state) disagrees with the policies they have chosen.

Founders: The men and women who were involved in creating the American nation during and after the American Revolution. Sometimes, the phrase is used to refer specifically to the men who participated in writing and ratifying the United States Constitution.

House of Representatives: Congress is divided into two halves: The House of Representatives and the Senate. The House is composed of representatives who are elected in each state. States do not all have the same number of representatives in the House. The big states get the most representatives and the small states get the least. Every state gets at least one representative, though.

King: The male ruler of a nation. Often, the King obtains his position because he was born into a certain family. The British King discussed in this book is King George III. He became King of Great Britain and Ireland after his grandfather, King George II, passed away.

President: The United States government is divided into three sections (usually called three "branches"): Executive, Legislative, and Judicial. The President is the head of the Executive branch. His job is to make sure that the laws are enforced. He also serves as Commander-in-Chief of the armed forces, and he is the leader in our relationships with other countries.

Republic: A republic is a self-governing society, just as a democracy is. However, more discussion and compromise are expected in a republic, and there are more protections for individual rights. Majority groups do not always get their way, especially when they are voting to hurt the interests of other people. Our Founders created a republic, not a democracy.

Self-governing: The ability of the people in a nation to make their own laws, usually through representatives that they have elected. They are ruled by themselves, not by someone else.

Senate: Congress is divided into two halves: The House of Representatives and the Senate. The Senate is composed of two people from each state. The size of your state does not matter in the Senate. Every state has the exact same number of Senators (two).

Taxes: A sum of money that a citizen is made to pay to the government. The government uses the money for its own maintenance or for other purposes such as national defense.

Tyranny: The use of power in a mean, unreasonable, or unfair way.

Notes and Sources

"We've used this system to pick all our Presidents."

The provisions for electing Presidents can be found in Article II, Section 1, Clauses 2 & 3 of the U.S. Constitution, but please note that a few small changes were made when the 12th Amendment was ratified in 1804. Under the original Article II provision, the person who obtained a majority of electors was elected President, while the second-place winner became Vice President. The 12th amendment separated these two elections. As it works today, electors cast one ballot for President and one ballot for Vice President. See chapter 3 of *Enlightened Democracy: The Case for the Electoral College.*

"First, people vote in their states."

The text describes the system as it operates today. Please also see the note below for "Do you know how states make this decision? Easy!"

"A democracy is a volcano . . . ."

Fisher Ames, Speech in the Convention of Massachusetts, on Biennial Elections (Jan. 1788), *in* 2 WORKS OF FISHER AMES 3, 7 (Seth Ames ed., 1854).

"[D]emocracy never lasts long. . . ."

Letter from John Adams to John Taylor (Apr. 15, 1814), *in* 6 THE WORKS OF JOHN ADAMS, SECOND PRESIDENT OF THE UNITED STATES 447, 484 (Charles Francis Adams ed., 2d prtg. 1969).

"A simple democracy . . . is one of the greatest of evils."

Letter from Benjamin Rush to John Adams (July 21, 1789), *in* 1 LETTERS OF BENJAMIN RUSH 522, 523 (L. H. Butterfield ed., 1951).

"Pure democracy . . . is very subject to caprice . . . ."

JOHN WITHERSPOON, *Lecture XII of Civil Society*, *in* AN ANNOTATED EDITION OF *LECTURES ON MORAL PHILOSOPHY* 140, 144 (Jack Scott ed., 1982).

"To secure the public good and private rights . . . ."

THE FEDERALIST NO. 10, at 75 (James Madison) (Clinton Rossiter ed., Signet Classic 2003) (1961).

"A Republic, if you can keep it."

WILLIAM G. CARR, THE OLDEST DELEGATE: FRANKLIN IN THE CONSTITUTIONAL CONVENTION 122 (1990) (citation omitted).

"The most populous States by combining . . . ."

JAMES MADISON, NOTES OF DEBATES IN THE FEDERAL CONVENTION OF 1787, at 307 (Adrienne Koch ed., W.W. Norton & Co. 1987) (1966).

"I do not, gentlemen, trust you. . . ."

Robert Yates, *Notes of the Secret Debates of the Federal Convention of 1787*, THE AVALON PROJECT: YALE LAW SCH., http://avalon.law.yale.edu/18th_century/yates.asp (last visited June 1, 2016).

"He will be the mere creature of the [Legislature] . . . ."

MADISON, *supra*, at 306.

"[T]he appointment of the Executive should either be . . . ."

MADISON, *supra*, at 327.

"Fortunately, the Founders worked out a compromise."

This compromise is often called the "Great Compromise" or the "Connecticut Compromise" (in deference to the Connecticut delegates who proposed it).

"Do you know how states make this decision? Easy!"

It's worth noting that states are not required to select their electors by means of a statewide popular vote. The Constitution gives the state legislature quite a bit of discretion in this area, simply providing that "Each State shall appoint, in such Manner as the Legislature thereof may direct, a Number of Electors . . . ." If a state legislature wants to select the electors on its own, without recourse to a popular vote, then the Constitution permits this decision. Indeed, in the first few presidential elections, some legislatures did exactly that. Of course, no state legislature is likely to do away with popular elections in this day and age. No doubt their constituents would be furious! See chapter 3 of *Enlightened Democracy*, supra.

"The candidate who wins the most votes in a state gets to be . . . ."

All states allocate their electors in a winner-take-all fashion, except Maine and Nebraska. Those two states instead give one elector to the winner of each of their congressional districts. Then they award their final two electors to the winner of their state popular votes.

"These electors have already promised to vote for . . . ."

Importantly, we are not expecting Republicans to keep a promise to vote for Democrats or vice versa. Each political party has its own slate of electors. In Texas, for example, the state Republican Party approves a slate of 38 electors. The state Democratic Party approves its own, separate slate of 38 people. If the Republican candidate wins the election, then the 38 Republican Texans will travel to the state capital and represent Texas in the Electoral College vote. If the Democratic candidate wins, then the 38 Democratic Texans will go instead.

"A President is elected if a majority of electors vote for him."

If no candidate gets a majority, then the presidential election moves to a back-up election process known as the Contingent Election. In that election, the House chooses a President from the top three presidential candidates. The Senate chooses a Vice President from the top two vice presidential candidates. In the House, each state delegation has one vote. In the Senate, each Senator gets one vote.

"Every once in a while, Presidents are elected because they got the most electors to vote for them . . . ."

At least two Presidents have been elected with an Electoral College win, but a popular vote loss: Benjamin Harrison (1888), and George W. Bush (2000). Some academics would add 1824 and 1876 to this list, but the popular vote tallies in those years were not entirely clear for reasons discussed in Chapter 15 of *Enlightened Democracy*, supra.

"When candidates forget this and focus too much on only one kind of voter, they always lose."

A great example of this dynamic is the 1888 election. Benjamin Harrison was elected that year with 233 electoral votes compared to Grover Cleveland's 168 electoral votes. Harrison won the electoral vote, even though Cleveland (barely) won the national popular vote. The distribution of votes explains the outcome. Cleveland's support was too focused on a handful of southern states. While he won landslide victories in six southern states, he was not as well received elsewhere. By contrast, Harrison did a better job of building a national coalition that spanned regions and states. His campaign reached out to a greater variety of people. The Electoral College rewarded Harrison's efforts to unify and penalized Cleveland's over-reliance on one type of voter. See chapter 16 of *Enlightened Democracy*, supra.

"They do poorly when they make some groups of people really mad at the other groups."

This is not to pretend that every presidential election year ends in perfect harmony! The 1860 election did culminate in a four-way race, after all. However, the incentives of our existing system are clear: Unify and bring people together for the greatest likelihood of success. Exhibit divisiveness or over-reliance on one type of voter and expect your political party and campaigns to suffer accordingly.

"Grover Cleveland finally figured out how to earn . . . . "

Ironically, he failed to win re-election in 1888 because his campaign was perceived as too focused on the South, per the note above.

"The mode of appointment of the Chief Magistrate . . . ."

THE FEDERALIST NO. 68, at 410 (Alexander Hamilton) (Clinton Rossiter ed., Signet Classic 2003) (1961).

Other Resources

Books

Tara Ross, *Enlightened Democracy: The Case for the Electoral College* (2d ed. 2012).

After The People Vote: A Guide to the Electoral College (John C. Fortier ed., 3d ed. 2004).

Judith Best, *The Case Against Direct Election of the President: A Defense of the Electoral College* (1975).

Judith A. Best, *The Choice of the People? Debating the Electoral College* (1996).

George Grant, *The Importance of the Electoral College* (2004).

Securing Democracy: Why We Have An Electoral College (Gary L. Gregg II ed., 2008).

Robert M. Hardaway, *The Electoral College and the Constitution: The Case for Preserving Federalism* (1994).

Websites

Tara Ross, *Electoral College Resources*
   http://www.taraross.com/category/electoral-college-resources/

Ashbrook Center at Ashland University, *Resources on the Electoral College*
   http://ashbrook.org/programs/citizens/electoral-college/

National Archives and Records Administration: *U.S. Electoral College Home*
   http://www.archives.gov/federal-register/electoral-college/

Save Our States
   http://www.saveourstates.com/